Eat your greens reds yellows and purples

Penguin Random House

Senior designer Sadie Thomas
Editors James Mitchem, Carrie Love
US editor Margaret Parrish
Editorial assistant Sophia Danielsson-Waters
Art direction for photography Charlotte Bull
Photographer Dave King
Food stylist Georgie Besterman
Nutritional consultant Fiona Hunter
Recipe consultant Lorna Rhodes
US consultant Kate Ramos
Senior producer Leila Green
Producer, Pre-Production Dragana Puvacic
Jacket designer Amy Keast
Jacket coordinator Francesca Young
Creative technical support Sonia Charbonnier
Managing editor Penny Smith
Managing art editor Gemma Glover
Art director Jane Bull
Publisher Mary Ling

First American Edition, 2016
Published in the United States by DK Publishing
1450 Broadway, Suite 801, New York, NY 10018

Copyright © 2016 Dorling Kindersley Limited
DK, a Division of Penguin Random House LLC
19 20   10 9 8 7 6 5 4
009–291661–May/16

A catalog record for this book is available from the
Library of Congress.
ISBN: 978–1–4654–5152–1
DK books are available at special discounts when purchased in bulk
for sales promotions, premiums, fundraising, or educational use.
For details, contact: DK Publishing Special
Markets, 1450 Broadway, Suite 801, New York, NY 10018
SpecialSales@dk.com

Printed in China
All images © Dorling Kindersley Limited
For further information see: www.dkimages.com

A WORLD OF IDEAS:
SEE ALL THERE IS KNOW

www.dk.com

THE MENU

GET COOKING

Here's a guide to the equipment used in this book. Obviously, you'll need only certain items for each recipe, so read through each one before you begin to make sure you have what you need.

KEY TO THE SYMBOLS USED IN THE RECIPES

PREP TIME
How long a recipe will take to prepare (includes chilling, etc.)

COOKING TIME
How much time each recipe will actually take to cook.

SERVES
How many people the recipe will serve, or how many portions it makes.

SAFETY
Take extra special care and ask an adult for help.

Large ovenproof dish

Pots (variety of sizes)

Lasagna pan

Mixing bowls

Baking sheets

Rimless baking sheet

Muffin pan

Baking pan

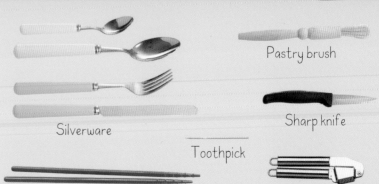

Silverware

Pastry brush

Sharp knife

Toothpick

Chopsticks

Garlic press

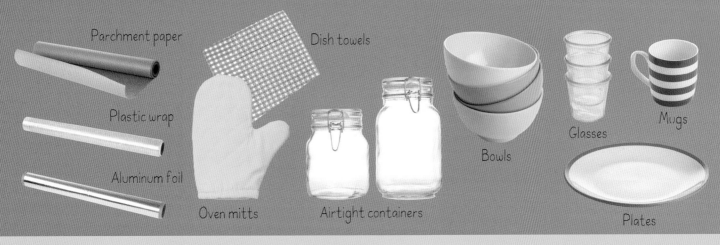

Parchment paper

Dish towels

Bowls

Glasses

Mugs

Plastic wrap

Aluminum foil

Oven mitts

Airtight containers

Plates

Saucepans (with lids)

Colander

Nonstick frying pan

Grill pan

Scales

Measuring spoons

Measuring cups

Pitcher

Grater

Wok

Sieve

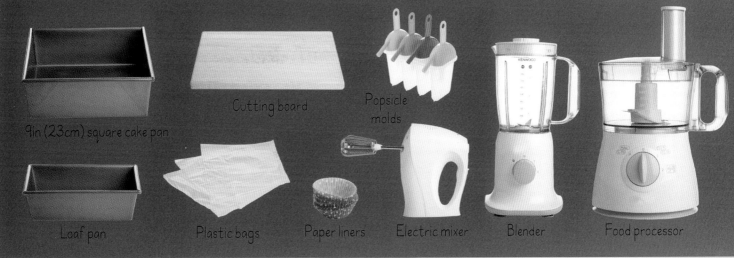

9in (23cm) square cake pan

Cutting board

Popsicle molds

Loaf pan

Plastic bags

Paper liners

Electric mixer

Blender

Food processor

Spatula

Serving spoon

Rolling pin

Peeler

Ladle

Wooden spoon

Rubber spatula

Potato masher

Whisk

5

EAT YOUR GREENS

GREEN food is packed with VITAMINS, FIBER, and other goodies that help keep your body healthy and strong. Some of these things are hard to find in other food, so the more peas, broccoli, spinach, and beans you eat, the better!

AND YOUR REDS

RED food can be a good source of vitamins that help protect your body's cells. Be sure to eat your fill of tomatoes, radishes, cherries, berries, and watermelon.

Vitamin A

Vitamin C

AND YOUR PURPLES

PURPLE food such as blackberries, blueberries, red cabbage, raisins, eggplants, plums, and grapes can contain chemicals that help protect your body from DISEASE and keep your heart healthy.

AND YOUR YELLOWS

YELLOW food usually contains lots of Vitamin A and C. By eating plenty of corn, lemons, bananas, peppers, melon, apricots, and pineapple, you will boost your body's IMMUNE SYSTEM, which is what makes sure you stay well.

AND YOUR ORANGES

ORANGE food such as carrots, sweet potatoes, squash, pumpkin, and—of course—oranges can contain something called CAROTENES. These are converted to Vitamin A, which help keeps your eyes, skin, hair, bones, and teeth in good shape.

Vitamin B

Vitamin C

EAT A RAINBOW

Meet the stars of the show! Fruits and veggies are packed with wonderful things your body needs. Every color is good in different ways—whether it's helping you grow big and strong, stopping you from getting sick, or giving you energy. So, don't just stop at one or two colors. Fill your plate with a rainbow of flavor!

Garlic

Pineapple

Onion

Potato

Avocado

Lime

Arugula

Kale

Leeks

Lemon

Yellow bell pepper

Peas

Green bell pepper

Broccoli

Bananas

Corn

Celery

Zucchini

Asparagus

Ginger

Scallions

Green beans

Green grapes

Spinach

Cucumber

Honeydew melon

Sweet potato

Grapefruits

How many have you TRIED?

Butternut squash

Tangerine

Chiles

Red bell pepper

Papayas

Strawberries

Apple

Blackberries

Blueberries

Peaches

Orange bell pepper

Raspberries

Cherries

Eggplant

Beet

Oranges

Carrot

Watermelon

Red cabbage

Apricot

Raisins

Red grapes

Pumpkin

Tomatoes

Red onion

Figs

Plum

9

PREPARING YOUR INGREDIENTS

Fruits and vegetables need a little love and care before they're ready to be used. There are lots of ways to prepare them, but these basic skills are bound to be useful again and again.

GINGER

TAKE A PIECE OF GINGER and use a teaspoon to scrape off the skin. Rub the ginger on a grater or cut it into slices.

POTATOES

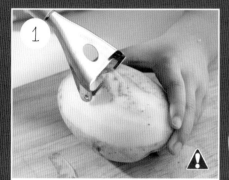

USE A PEELER to remove the skin, then rinse the potatoes in cold water. You can prepare sweet potatoes the same way.

CAREFULLY CUT THE POTATO into whichever shape you need. This could be little chunks, wedges, slices, or batons (for fries).

BROCCOLI

HOLD THE BROCCOLI by the stalk. Carefully go around the stalk with a knife, trimming off the florets (little trees). Then slice the stalk.

GARLIC

FIRMLY PUSH DOWN on a bulb of garlic to break it into segments (cloves). Press down on the cloves with a knife to loosen the papery peel.

PLACE THE CLOVES in a garlic crusher and squeeze. If you need slices, ask an adult for help, since garlic has to be sliced very thinly.

CARROTS

USE A PEELER to remove the skin, then either grate or cut the carrots into rounds or batons (little rectangles that look like fries).

AVOCADOS

1 CAREFULLY CUT AROUND the outside of the avocado, then twist the two halves to separate them.

2 USE A SPOON to remove the pit, then either peel off the skin or scoop out the flesh.

TOMATOES

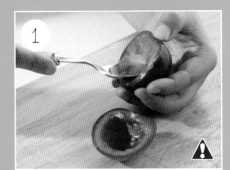

1 CAREFULLY CUT your tomatoes in half, then use a spoon to scoop out all the seeds.

BELL PEPPERS

1 CUT THE BELL PEPPER in half from top to bottom. Remove the stalk, seeds, and white pith.

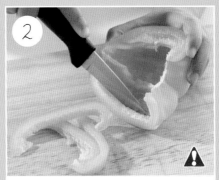

2 CAREFULLY SLICE the bell pepper into strips, chunks, or cubes, depending on the recipe.

ZUCCHINI

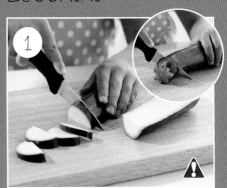

1 TRIM BOTH ENDS of the zucchini and either cut into rounds, or cut in half lengthwise, then slice into half-moon shapes.

ONIONS

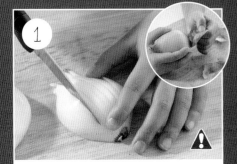

1 PEEL THE ONION and slice it in half from root to stem. Make several slices toward the root, but don't cut all the way to the end.

2 MAKE SIDEWAYS CUTS toward the root—once near the bottom and once near the top.

3 HOLDING THE ONION together, cut down across the cuts. This will separate the onion into little cubes. This is known as dicing.

MEET THE GREENS

HOWDY, ALL! First up, there's bold broccoli, then there's amazing avocado, followed by luscious lime, powerful peas, great green beans, and last, but not least, strong spinach! Greens are good for your overall health and, in particular, your blood and heart.

We're the
GREEN TEAM

Broccoli contains almost as much Vitamin C as oranges.

I'm high in antioxidants, which help to slow down wear and tear on your body's cells.

GREENS ARE GOOD

There's a reason that people are always saying "eat your greens." Green food is often full of Vitamin K and other goodies that your body needs to stay healthy. (Sadly, this doesn't include green candy!)

B vitamins

Cooked spinach contains LESS nutrition than raw spinach, but it's still healthy!

Scallions are also called green onions. They are full of goodness.

Healthy fats

Grapes are a lovely sweet treat that also give your body what it needs.

AVOCADO
Sometimes called "alligator pears," avocados are filled with healthy fats.

BROCCOLI

Not only is broccoli one of the healthiest foods you can eat, but it's also much tastier than people give it credit for! It's packed with amazing ANTIOXIDANTS that can help protect the cells in your body from all kinds of bad stuff.

Curly kale is known as a SUPERFOOD.

Vitamin K.

GREEN BEANS

Great green beans are a source of healthy, natural chemicals found in plants (phytochemicals). If you cook green beans for too long they will lose a lot of their benefits. Plus, no one likes a soggy bean!

Green beans are tasty in stir-fries!

Vitamin C

ASPARAGUS
Vitamin K is good for the bloodstream. These spears are full of it.

I'm also a good source of POTASSIUM.

PEAS are great, whether they're fresh or frozen.

SPINACH AND PHYLLO TARTS

Superhero spinach to the rescue! These simple tarts are easy to make for an afternoon snack or as part of a main meal. Crumble feta cheese on each tart to add flavor and extra dairy to your diet.

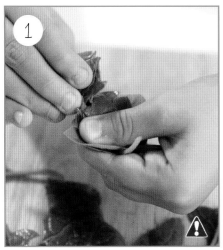

1

PREHEAT THE OVEN to 350°F (180°C). Brush a muffin pan with oil and set aside. Gently tear the spinach and the basil into pieces.

2

IN A LARGE MIXING BOWL, beat the cream cheese, egg, and grated cheese until smooth. Season with salt and pepper, then stir in the spinach.

3

CAREFULLY CUT the phyllo dough into 16 squares measuring 5in (12.5cm) each. Brush the squares with a little olive oil.

I help fight disease. I also make you grow big and strong. Spinach rules!

INGREDIENTS

- 1 tbsp olive oil
- 9oz (250g) baby spinach leaves, washed
- 2 tbsp fresh basil
- 9oz (250g) softened cream cheese
- 1 large egg, beaten
- 1oz (25g) Cheddar or vegetarian Parmesan cheese, grated
- Salt and freshly ground black pepper
- 9oz (250g) phyllo dough
- 1¾oz (50g) feta cheese, crumbled (optional)

15 mins | 20 mins | Makes 8

PLACE ONE SQUARE on top of another dough square at an angle to form the base of each tart. Repeat this process with the rest of the sheets. You should have enough to make 8 tarts.

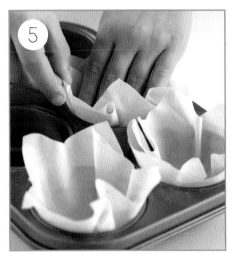

GENTLY PLACE the dough sheets in the muffin pan. Push them into the corners to make them fit.

SPOON THE MIXTURE into the shells and smooth it down with the back of the spoon. Bake them for 25 minutes, until the filling has set and the dough is golden brown.

BLACK BEAN AND GUACAMOLE
QUESADILLA

The humble quesadilla (kay-sa-dee-ya) originated in Mexico. It is either a flour or corn tortilla that is filled with yummy ingredients and pan-fried. Here we have used black beans and guacamole, but you can make up your own fillings.

Not only does lime juice stop avocados from turning brown, but it's also full of Vitamin C. Sailors used to eat limes to prevent a disease called scurvy.

Avocados are full of good things such as Vitamin E, which helps to keep the cells in your body happy and healthy.

EAT ME before someone else does!

5 mins   5 mins   Serves 2

INGREDIENTS

- 1 tbsp olive oil
- 1 onion, chopped
- 1 clove garlic, crushed

- 14oz (400g) can black beans, drained
- Salt and freshly ground black pepper
- 1 avocado
- 1 tsp lime juice
- 1 red onion, finely chopped
- 1 tomato, seeded and finely chopped
- 1 tbsp cilantro, finely chopped

- 2 flour (or corn) tortillas
- 1oz (25g) grated Cheddar cheese

1 HEAT THE OIL in a pan and add the onion and garlic. Cook gently for a few minutes, then add the beans. Season and cook for 3 minutes more.

2 CAREFULLY CUT the avocado in half. Remove the pit and scoop out the flesh. Place it in a mixing bowl with the lime juice.

3 MIX IN THE RED ONION, tomatoes, and cilantro and season well with salt and pepper. Mash everything together using a potato masher or fork.

4 SPREAD THE beans and guacamole on a tortilla and scatter the cheese on top. Place in a warm frying pan over medium heat and put the second tortilla on top.

5 PRESS DOWN with a spatula and cook for 2–3 minutes, until the tortilla is crispy and the cheese is melting.

6 ASK AN ADULT to invert the tortilla onto a plate and slide it back into the pan so that the other side can cook for 2 minutes more.

LEAFY GREEN SALAD

Build up your own veggie army with this fresh green salad. Asparagus, broccoli, and green beans are packed with antioxidants, the wonderful warriors that fight "free radicals," which can harm the body's cells.

SNAP OFF THE BOTTOM part of the asparagus spears and discard them. Cut the rest of the spears into segments.

10 mins

5 mins

Serves 4

INGREDIENTS
- 3½oz (100g) asparagus
- 3½oz (100g) green beans, trimmed and halved
- ¾ cup fresh peas
- 3½oz (100g) broccoli, chopped
- 5½oz (150g) green leaves (baby spinach, arugula, watercress)
- 4in (10cm) piece of cucumber, halved lengthwise and sliced

DRESSING
- 2 tsp white wine vinegar
- 3 tbsp extra virgin olive oil
- 1 tbsp lemon juice
- 1 tsp honey
- 1 tsp pesto

The Vitamin K in asparagus spears is good for your bones.

COOK THE BEANS in boiling water for 2 minutes. Add the asparagus, peas, and broccoli. Simmer for 3 minutes. Drain, rinse in cold water, then drain again.

PLACE ALL THE DRESSING ingredients in a bowl. Whisk with a fork until they have all blended together.

PLACE THE SALAD LEAVES and cucumber in a large bowl. Add the cooked vegetables and drizzle the dressing over the top. Toss and serve.

Oops, I dropped it!

Broccoli is great for you. It contains nutrients that help keep your heart healthy, and it is also full of vitamins.

ZUCCHINI FRITTATA

This frittata is tasty eaten hot or cold. The eggs are full of protein, which helps build and repair your body, and the fiber in the veggies keeps your digestive system working properly.

POWERFUL protein tower

Zucchini contains POTASSIUM, which is good for controlling blood pressure.

Potatoes are a great source of energy.

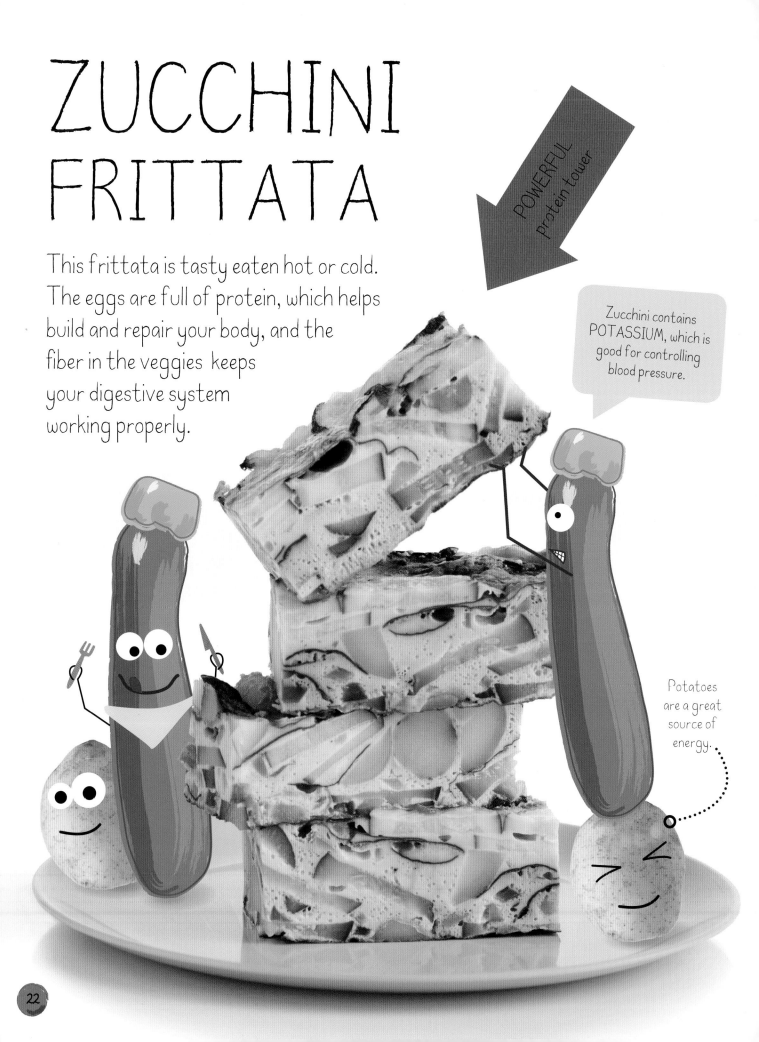

25 mins

 40 mins

 Serves 8

INGREDIENTS

- 14oz (400g) new potatoes
- 4 tbsp butter
- 1 large onion, finely chopped
- 3 zucchini, thinly sliced
- 1 green bell pepper, seeded and chopped
- 3½oz (100g) spinach
- 8 eggs
- 2½oz (75g) vegetarian Parmesan cheese
- 1 tbsp fresh mint leaves, chopped
- Freshly ground black pepper

All bell peppers start out green and change color and flavor as they ripen.

1 COOK THE POTATOES in a saucepan of boiling water for 15 minutes, or until tender. Drain and let cool, then cut into chunks.

2 MELT THE BUTTER in a nonstick pan and cook the onion on low heat until soft. Add the zucchini and bell pepper. Cook for 3 minutes, stirring occasionally.

3 PREHEAT THE BROILER. While it's heating, add the spinach and potatoes and cook for 5 minutes, until the spinach is wilted.

4 CRACK THE EGGS into a bowl and add the Parmesan, mint, and a pinch of pepper. Use a fork to mix everything together.

5 POUR THE EGG MIXTURE into the pan and set the heat to low. Cook for 5 minutes, until the eggs are almost set.

6 PLACE THE PAN under the preheated broiler and cook until brown on top—about 5 minutes. Remove and let cool before cutting into slices.

GREEN BEAN STIR-FRY

Stir-frying is a way of cooking that helps vegetables keep their nutrients and stay crunchy. This dish is packed with healthy veggies, and the coconut makes it extra yummy.

Broccoli is sometimes called a superfood because it's so full of goodness.

BEAN SPROUTS are very filling.

24

INGREDIENTS

- ⅔ cup shredded coconut, unsweetened
- 2 tbsp sunflower oil
- 6 scallions, chopped
- 1 garlic clove, sliced
- 1 fennel bulb, sliced, core removed
- 5½oz (150g) small broccoli florets
- 3½oz (100g) green beans, trimmed
- 1 tbsp rice vinegar
- 2 tbsp soy sauce
- 3½oz (100g) bean sprouts
- 1 tbsp fresh cilantro, chopped
- 7oz (200g) whole wheat noodles
- 1 tbsp sesame seeds
- ⅔ cup unsalted cashews, roasted

Broccoli and green beans are great together.

1 PLACE THE COCONUT in a pitcher of warm water. Cover and leave for 20 minutes, then strain through a sieve and reserve the coconut and the liquid.

2 HEAT THE OIL in a wok or frying pan and cook the scallions, garlic, fennel, and broccoli for about 2 minutes, stirring occasionally.

3 ADD THE BEANS and cook for 4–5 minutes. Add the vinegar, soy sauce, and ¼ cup of reserved coconut water. Mix, then cook for 1 minute. Take off the heat.

4 ADD THE BEAN SPROUTS and the drained coconut. Sprinkle the cilantro on top and mix everything together well.

5 COOK AND DRAIN the noodles as instructed on the package. Spoon a portion into each of your serving bowls.

6 SPRINKLE SESAME seeds and cashews on top of your stir-fry, then spoon the mixture on top of the noodles. This will give the dish a crunchy texture.

GREEN SMOOTHIE

Grapes are just glorious. They are loaded with goodness and help your blood move around your body. Bananas are equally brilliant—they contain potassium that keeps your heart beating strong. Mix them with spinach and you've got the best combo for a tasty, healthy smoothie.

5 mins   0 mins   Makes 2–4

INGREDIENTS

- 1 small or ½ large banana
- ¾ cup green grapes
- 2oz (60g) baby spinach
- ⅔ cup milk
(Use almond milk if preferred)
- 1 tbsp honey
- 1 tbsp almond or peanut butter
- Handful of ice cubes

1

PEEL THE BANANA and break it into chunks. Put into a blender along with the grapes.

2

ADD THE SPINACH, milk, honey, nut butter, and a handful of ice cubes to the blender.

3

BLEND THE MIXTURE until smooth. If it's too thick or not chilled enough, just add a few cubes of ice and blend again.

26

You can adapt this recipe to get a different flavor. Try adding a large pinch of ground cinnamon or even a few fresh mint leaves.

My friend spinach is rich in vitamins, which help to keep your blood healthy.

MEET THE REDS

WE'RE THE RADICAL REDS, and we're known for being bright, cheery, and bursting with flavor. From small to large, we include tart raspberries, sweet strawberries, juicy tomatoes, sweet red onions, and rosy red bell peppers. The darker and richer the red, the more nutrients we contain.

INTENSE and flavorful.

Reach for THE REDS.

Red onions help to keep your heart healthy, as well as reducing high blood pressure.

29

REACH FOR THE REDS

Red may be the color of fire and anger, but it's hard to be angry when you're chomping on these vibrant, tasty fruits and vegetables! In fact, the more you eat, the happier (and healthier!) you'll be.

Always eat the peel of a red apple—it's where most of the goodness is!

CHERRIES contain melatonin, which can help you to have a good night's sleep.

RASPBERRIES
Soft, springy, and delicious, raspberries are one of the sweetest fruits around.

RED BELL PEPPER

Red bell peppers are even better than their green and yellow cousins. This is because the red ones contain more nutrients. Eat them raw, or cook them in a tasty dish—no matter what, they'll lend a helping hand to protect your heart and eyes.

Go ahead, get your REDS!

TOMATOES

All types of tomato contain lovely lycopene. Lycopene is what gives tomatoes their red color, but more importantly, it protects the cells in your body and boosts your immune system. You get more lycopene from cooked tomatoes than raw ones.

WATERMELONS contain lots of water and fiber, which help your digestion.

Lots of
LYCOPENE

CHILES can be so spicy they'll make you sweat. But that's okay! Herbs and spices add lots of flavor.

RED ONION

Both red and white onions contain plenty of a mineral called SULFUR. It's a great mineral—it really helps your blood and can also make your hair healthy and glossy.

Super
SULFUR

GRAPEFRUITS can taste fairly bitter, but they're full of Vitamin C.

I'm a fantastic STRAWBERRY. I start to lose my nutrients as soon as I'm picked, so eat me ASAP!

RED PEPPER HUMMUS

Red bell peppers are naturally sweet, and are seriously delicious as an ingredient in a hummus dip. They help add to the texture and the taste. Red bell peppers are also loaded with Vitamin C.

CHICKPEAS are one of the best sources of protein out there.

INGREDIENTS

- 2 red bell peppers, plus extras for serving
- ¾ cup canned chickpeas, drained
- 1 tsp paprika
- 1 clove garlic, peeled
- Juice of 1 lemon
- 1 tbsp tahini
- 3 tbsp olive oil
- Salt and freshly ground black pepper
- 1 large carrot, peeled, for serving
- 2 celery ribs, for serving
- ½ cucumber, for serving
- 2 slices of whole-grain pita bread, sliced

20 mins   5 mins   Serves 2

Garlic is a strong-flavored vegetable. It helps to keep your heart healthy.

1 PREHEAT THE BROILER. Carefully cut the peppers into quarters and remove all of the pith and seeds.

2 LINE A BAKING SHEET with foil. Place the bell peppers on it with the skin side facing up. Broil them for 5 minutes, until the skins have blackened.

3 PUT THE BELL PEPPERS in a bag and seal it. Wait for 10 minutes, until the bell peppers are cool, then peel off the skins. They should come off easily.

4 PUT THE BELL PEPPERS, chickpeas, paprika, garlic, lemon juice, tahini, and olive oil into a food processor and blend until smooth. Season to taste.

5 CAREFULLY CUT THE CARROTS, celery, red bell peppers, and cucumber into sticks.

6 SPOON THE HUMMUS into a bowl and serve with the vegetable sticks and toasted pita bread.

33

TOMATO SOUP

This is classic comfort food for when it's cold outside. Tomatoes are packed with Vitamin C, Vitamin A, and potassium. Did you know that tomatoes are actually a fruit, not a vegetable?

20 mins | 35 mins | Serves 2–4

INGREDIENTS

- ¼ cup olive oil
- 1 small onion, chopped
- 1 small carrot, chopped
- 2 ribs celery, chopped
- 1 garlic clove, crushed
- 1 tbsp all-purpose flour
- 14oz (400g) can chopped tomatoes
- 1 tbsp tomato paste
- 1 tbsp fresh thyme leaves, chopped
- 1¾ cup vegetable stock
- A pinch of sugar
- Salt and freshly ground pepper

Eat me, and I will help to keep your heart healthy.

I'm packed with VITAMIN C.

Tomatoes also contain something called lycopene, which is a powerful antioxidant that helps prevent disease. Lycopene gives tomatoes their deep red color.

1 HEAT THE OLIVE OIL in a small pan over medium heat, and then add the onion, carrot, and celery.

2 COOK THE ONION, carrot, and celery for about 5 minutes, until they soften, then stir in the garlic and flour and cook for another minute.

3 ADD THE CANNED TOMATOES, tomato paste, thyme, stock, and sugar. Bring the mixture to a boil, then reduce to low heat and simmer for 25 minutes.

4 REMOVE THE SOUP from the heat and let it cool. Ladle it into a blender and blend until smooth. Pour back into a pan and reheat before serving. Season with salt and freshly ground pepper.

TOMATO
AND ONION TARTS

These tarts are surprisingly filling. When cooked, puff pastry rises and leaves air pockets inside, making it light and fluffy. Puff pastry can be used for savory or sweet dishes.

Help me sprinkle more of these basil leaves on top. They add to the flavor!

Totally tasty
TARTS

10 mins   20 mins   Serves 6

INGREDIENTS

- 13oz (375g) store-bought puff pastry
- 9oz (250g) cherry tomatoes
- 9oz (250g) ricotta cheese
- 2 large eggs, beaten
- 2 tbsp basil, freshly chopped
- 1oz (25g) vegetarian Parmesan (or mozzarella) cheese, grated
- Salt and freshly ground black pepper
- 1 red onion, sliced

Cherry tomatoes are high in Vitamin A and Vitamin B6.

PREHEAT THE OVEN to 400°F (200°C). On a lightly floured surface, roll the pastry out into a rectangle measuring 10 x 15in (25 x 38cm).

USE A KNIFE to cut six equal squares of pastry, then score a ½in (1cm) border around the edges. Transfer the squares onto a greased baking sheet.

SLICE THE CHERRY TOMATOES in half. If you have one, a serrated knife makes the job easier.

Scatter fresh basil leaves on top of each tart.

IN A LARGE MIXING BOWL, combine the ricotta, eggs, basil, and Parmesan (or mozzarella). Season with salt and pepper.

SPREAD THE MIXTURE on the squares, making sure to stay inside the borders. Scatter the tomatoes and onion on top and bake for 20 minutes, or until golden.

VEGGIE LASAGNA

A hearty, lovely lasagna is packed tight with good, colorful veggies. The pretty, purple eggplant adds to the texture, contains Vitamins B1 and B6, and is filled with fiber.

They may make you cry, but onions really help your health. Red ones are the sweetest.

Bell peppers contain lots of Vitamins A and C. Did you know that Vitamin A can help your eyesight?

50 mins | 1hr 15 mins | Serves 6

INGREDIENTS

- 2 large red onions, peeled
- 2 zucchini
- 2 large carrots, peeled
- 4 red bell peppers, seeded
- 6oz (175g) mushrooms, halved or quartered, depending on the size
- 1 medium eggplant
- 2 garlic cloves, crushed
- 2 tbsp rosemary, chopped
- ¼ cup olive oil
- 14oz (400g) can of chopped tomatoes
- 1 tbsp tomato paste
- 1 tsp dried oregano
- Salt and freshly ground black pepper
- 4 tbsp unsalted butter
- ¼ cup all-purpose flour
- 2 cups warm milk
- 3½oz (100g) vegetarian Parmesan cheese, grated
- 10 no-cook lasagna sheets

PREHEAT THE OVEN to 425°F (220°C). Cut the onions, zucchini, carrots, peppers, mushrooms, and eggplant into chunks.

PLACE THE CUT veggies in an ovenproof dish. Add the garlic, rosemary, and oil. Toss, then roast for 30 minutes. Turn the vegetables over halfway through.

COOK THE TOMATOES, tomato paste, and oregano over low heat for 15 minutes. Season and stir in the vegetables, then take off the heat.

MELT THE BUTTER over low heat and stir in the flour. Cook for 1 minute, then slowly whisk in the milk a little at a time until it has thickened. Add half the cheese.

REDUCE THE OVEN temperature to 375°F (190°C). Spoon one-third of the vegetable mixture into a lasagna dish and top with 3 lasagna sheets.

ADD ANOTHER THIRD of the vegetable mix and lasagna sheets. Top with half of the sauce, then the remaining vegetables.

LAY ON THE FINAL lasagna sheets, then spread the remaining sauce on top. Sprinkle on the remaining cheese and bake for 35 minutes, until golden.

VERY BERRY PLUM PIE

Berries and plums have their own natural sugars that bring a delicious, sweet flavor to this puffy pie. Serve with a scoop of ice cream to take this treat to the next level.

INGREDIENTS

- 1lb 2oz (500g) store-bought pie dough
- Flour, for dusting
- 1 egg, beaten

- 1lb 6oz (650g) mixed berries—raspberries and strawberries
- 2 tbsp granulated sugar
- 2 tbsp cornstarch
- 7oz (200g) plums, pitted and cut into quarters
- Confectioners' sugar, for dusting

Strawberries are great. One handful contains as much Vitamin C as a whole orange!

1 PREHEAT THE OVEN to 400°F (200°C). On a lightly floured surface, roll out the pie dough until it's about ¼in (5mm) thick.

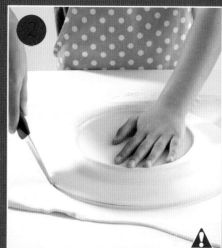

2 LAY A 10in (25cm) PLATE on the dough and cut around it. Move the circle onto a baking sheet and brush all over the surface with a little beaten egg.

3 COMBINE THE BERRIES, sugar, cornstarch, and plums in a mixing bowl. Gently toss to coat, being careful not to crush the fruit.

SPOON THE FRUIT in the middle of the dough, leaving a 3in (7.5cm) border around the outside. Scrunch up the edges and bring them toward the center, leaving the middle uncovered.

PLACE IN THE FRIDGE for 30 minutes to chill. Brush the crust with the leftover beaten egg, then place the pie in the oven.

BAKE THE PIE for 30 minutes, until golden brown, rotating half way through cooking. Allow 30 minutes to cool, then dust with confectioners' sugar and serve.

MEET THE PURPLES

PERFECT AND PROUD, the purples are happy
to tell you just how wonderful they are and
how they can help prevent you from becoming sick.
This group includes awesome eggplants,
brilliant blackberries, bold beets, great grapes,
breathtaking blueberries, and remarkable raisins.

Aren't we
PRETTY?!

Pick the
PURPLES

I help to increase
immunity, improve
heart health, and lower
the risk of disease.

43

PICK UP THE PURPLES

Fruits and veggies that are purple and dark blue are linked to keeping the HEART healthy and the BRAIN functioning at its best. They also help protect the body from disease, improve MEMORY, and increase blood circulation.

BLACKBERRIES
These berries are high in fiber, which aids digestion. They are also full of Vitamin K, which promotes good bone health.

FIGS
This sweet little fruit is a great source of fiber, vitamins, and MINERALS.

PURPLE GRAPES contain powerful ANTIOXIDANTS.

EGGPLANT

Not only is this mighty warrior full of fiber, but it also boasts high levels of Vitamin C. It is healthy because it's low in fat and can help to remove excess iron in the body. It might sound surprising, but eggplants are actually a very large berry—so they're fruit, not veggies.

I'm great at soaking up lots of other great flavors.

BLUEBERRIES

These delicious berries are high in fiber as well as Vitamin E and C. They're full of wonderful antioxidants that protect you from disease, and research has shown that they boost brain activity.

PLUMS are full of Vitamin B.

PURPLE CABBAGE
This veggie is commonly called "red cabbage." It's really high in Vitamin A.

RAISINS
Did you know that raisins are dried grapes? They're tasty to eat raw.

Fiber

BEETS

Although they can be eaten raw, beets are usually cooked or pickled before being eaten. The leaves are rich in calcium, iron, and vitamins and the roots are a source of FOLIC ACID, which can help your body build new cells.

Vitamin C

FRUITY RAISIN GRANOLA

Breakfast is the most important meal of the day, and a great way to get a healthy energy boost. Raisins and berries are high in fiber. They are a fantastic way to kick-start your morning.

Blackberries have their own natural sweeteners, and they provide you with lots of Vitamin C.

Yum, yum, yum!

⊙ 5 mins   🕐 30 mins   🍽 Serves 8-10

INGREDIENTS

• ¾ cup mixed nuts (hazelnuts, walnuts, almonds)

• 3¾ cups rolled oats

• ½ cup pumpkin seeds

• ½ cup sunflower seeds

• 2 tbsp sunflower oil

• ½ cup honey

• ¾ cup raisins

• Blackberries, to serve

• Milk or yogurt, to serve

1

PREHEAT THE OVEN to 325°F (160°C). Put the nuts in a plastic bag and crush them with a rolling pin. In a large mixing bowl, combine the nuts, oats, and seeds.

2

IN A SMALL PITCHER, mix together the oil and honey, then pour it into the bowl of oats and seeds. Use a spoon to stir the mixture until it's well combined.

3

SPOON THE MIXTURE onto 2 baking sheets in a single layer, then bake in the oven for 15 minutes. Turn the mixture over and bake for an additional 15 minutes.

4

LET THE MIXTURE COOL, then pour into a bowl. Mix in the raisins and transfer into an airtight container to store. Serve in a bowl with yogurt and blackberries.

RAINBOW SALAD

All the colors in this book are shown off in this signature salad. Have fun building the layers that make up a beautiful and edible rainbow. Packed with vitamins, protein, and plenty of fiber, it's sure to become a family favorite.

25 mins 5 mins Serves 4

INGREDIENTS

- 2 tsp sesame oil
- 2 tsp rice vinegar
- 1 tbsp soy sauce
- 2 tsp honey
- 2 tbsp extra virgin olive oil
- 14oz (400g) tofu (one block)
- 1⅓ cups freshly shelled peas, or frozen peas, thawed
- Small handful mint leaves, torn
- 12 cherry tomatoes, halved
- 2 carrots, 7oz (200g), peeled and grated
- 1 yellow and 1 orange bell pepper, cut into strips
- 2 beets, 7oz (200g), peeled and grated
- Mixed salad leaves
- 1 tbsp toasted sesame seeds

You can make these salads ahead of time and take them on a picnic. They're perfect!

Beat the winter blues with beets. They're full of Vitamin C, so can help you to get over a cold more quickly.

Layers of GOODNESS

1

TO MAKE THE DRESSING, place the sesame oil, rice vinegar, soy sauce, honey, and 1 tbsp extra virgin olive oil in a sealable jar and shake until well mixed.

2

PLACE THE TOFU on a plate lined with paper towels. Place more paper towels and a cutting board on top. Leave for 15 minutes to help squeeze out any liquid.

3

CUT THE TOFU into 1in (2.5cm) cubes. Heat the remaining olive oil in a frying pan ready to cook the tofu.

4

ASK AN ADULT to cook the tofu over medium heat until it has browned on all sides. This will take about 5 minutes.

5

MAKE UP THE LAYERS of salad in a glass or jar. Begin with peas and mint, then add a layer of tomatoes, carrots, and yellow and orange bell peppers.

6

ADD A LAYER OF beets, tofu, and salad leaves. When you're ready to eat, add a little of the dressing, shake to combine, then top with the sesame seeds.

EGGPLANT
AND TOMATO BAKE

Dig into the layers of delicious goodness. The main ingredients that make this recipe are excellent eggplants and terrific tomatoes. Did you know that eggplants and tomatoes are both fruits?

Join us in our healthy feast. Eggplants are high in fiber and contain potassium.

Super-tasty TOPPING

30 mins 1 hr Serves 4

INGREDIENTS

- 4 tbsp extra virgin olive oil
- 1 medium onion, finely chopped
- 2 garlic cloves, finely chopped

- 2 x 14oz (400g) cans chopped tomatoes
- 1 tsp dried oregano
- 1 tsp sugar
- 2 medium eggplants, about 1lb 5oz (600g)
- Salt and freshly ground black pepper

- 3½oz (100g) grated mozzarella cheese

Eggplants are called aubergines in the UK.

PREHEAT THE OVEN to 375°F (190°C). Heat 1 tbsp of oil in a pan and cook the onion for 5 minutes. Add the garlic and cook for another minute.

ADD THE TOMATOES to the pan, then add the oregano and sugar and season with salt and pepper. Bring to a simmer and cook for 20 minutes.

CUT THE EGGPLANT into slices ¼in (5mm) thick. Brush the eggplant slices on each side with the remaining oil and season with salt and pepper.

HEAT A GRILL PAN, then working in batches over medium heat, brown the eggplants for 2–3 minutes on each side until tender. Set aside.

DIVIDE A THIRD of the tomato sauce into 4 dishes, then add 3–4 slices of eggplant. Repeat this process then finish with a layer of sauce on the top.

SCATTER THE CHEESE over the top. Bake in the oven for 25 minutes or until the tops are golden brown and bubbling.

51

LAYERED BERRY CHEESECAKES

Juicy blueberries and blackberries go really well with the crumbly, crushed cookies in this dish. These cheesecakes are best when very cold, so only take them out of the fridge just before you're ready to serve them.

1 hr 20 mins   5 mins   Serves 4

INGREDIENTS

- 10oz (300g) blueberries
- 9oz (250g) blackberries
- 2 tbsp granulated sugar
- 9oz (250g) cream cheese
- 1 cup crème fraiche
- 1 tsp vanilla extract
- 3½ oz (100g) oat cookies, crushed

Chilled and RELAXED

Blueberries and blackberries both contain natural chemicals that can help to protect you from disease.

PLACE TWO-THIRDS of the berries and 1 tbsp of sugar in a medium pan. Cover and cook over low heat for 5 minutes. Stir in the remaining berries and let cool.

BEAT THE REMAINING 1 tbsp sugar, cream cheese, crème fraîche, and vanilla extract in a bowl. Do this until the mixture is soft and creamy.

START TO LAYER the cheesecakes. In glasses or a jar, create a layer of berry sauce, then the cream cheese mixture, then the cookies. Repeat until you're finished.

DOT THE REMAINING fresh berries on top, then place the cheesecakes into the fridge for an hour to let them set. Share them with your friends!

MEET THE YELLOWS

Hi, there! We're good at all kinds of things, but we're best known for our ability to aid brain function and help with digestion. The yellow clan is made up of tasty bananas, powerful pineapples, juicy yellow bell peppers, scrumptious corn, zingy lemons, and, of course... the humble potato.

Yummy YELLOWS

Bright and BOLD

We increase your immunity, give you healthy skin, and help to prevent heart disease.

SAY YES TO YELLOWS

It's easy to feel mellow if you eat lots of yellow. The outsides may look sunny and powerful, but it's the insides that have the real power—the power to boost your immune system, that is!

PEACHES are naturally sweet and succulent. They're perfect with cereal or in a smoothie.

BELL PEPPERS start off green, then change color as they ripen. All the colors taste a bit different.

You can do so much with POTATOES, but it's often healthiest to bake or boil them. They fill you up and are a good source of energy.

SUPER spud

LEMONS

Lemons bring vibrant flavor to a dish, and they also bring lots of Vitamin C to your body. Sailors used to eat lemons to avoid a disease called scurvy.

HONEYDEW MELON is yummy at breakfast or as dessert.

BANANAS

According to scientists, bananas make you happy! This is because they contain amino acids that boost your serotonin—a chemical that makes you feel happy. Bananas also contain a special kind of fiber that encourages friendly bacteria in the gut.

CORN

Crunchy yellow corn is a brain food. It contains Vitamin B1, which is also known as thiamine. Thiamine is a fantastic memory booster, and it can improve your everyday thinking—so eat corn before you do your homework!

Tasty and TROPICAL

PINEAPPLES
Spiked on the outside, but sweet on the inside, pineapples take over a year to grow. Good things come to those who wait!

For thousands of years people have used GARLIC as a way to prevent illnesses. Cook with it the next time you have a cold!

PEPPER
AND QUINOA SALAD

INGREDIENTS

- 3 yellow bell peppers, seeded and chopped
- 1 medium red onion, thickly sliced
- 2 zucchini, halved lengthwise and sliced
- 8oz (225g) small cauliflower florets
- 12 cherry tomatoes
- 2 tbsp olive oil
- Salt and freshly ground black pepper
- 1 cup quinoa
- 1¼ cups vegetable stock
- Handful of basil leaves, chopped
- Handful of parsley leaves, chopped

This healthy salad contains such a variety of colorful ingredients. Quinoa is a healthy seed that's high in protein and contains fiber. If you can't find quinoa, couscous will work just as well.

PUSH, PUSH. Get it to the dinner table!

1 PREHEAT THE OVEN to 400°F (200°C). Put the peppers, onions, zucchini, cauliflower, and tomatoes in a roasting pan. Coat with oil. Season with salt and pepper.

2 ROAST THE VEGGIES in the oven for 20 minutes. While they're roasting, place the quinoa in a sieve. Rinse it under cold water so the quinoa doesn't taste bitter.

3 POUR THE QUINOA into a saucepan and add a pinch of salt. Stir over medium heat for 1 minute so the water evaporates and the quinoa toasts slightly.

The herbs add FLAVOR

POUR THE VEGETABLE STOCK into the pan and bring to a boil. Reduce it to a simmer, then cover and let the quinoa cook for 15 minutes.

REMOVE FROM THE HEAT and leave it covered for another 5 minutes to rest. This is an important step, since it will make the quinoa fluffy instead of soggy.

TRANSFER THE QUINOA into a large bowl and fluff it up with a fork. Add the roasted vegetables along with the fresh basil and parsley. Serve warm or cold.

BEAN AND CORN BAKE

This is an incredibly satisfying meal that's similar to the Greek dish moussaka. The creamy egg and yogurt mixture creates a delicious and fluffy topping. Serve with a salad to add extra colors from the food rainbow.

Cannellini beans are full of fiber and protein. Every cell in your body needs protein.

Yellow food, such as corn, helps your skin and eyes stay healthy.

15 mins   35 mins   Serves 4–6

INGREDIENTS

- 1 tbsp olive oil
- 1 onion, finely chopped
- 2 x 14oz (400g) cans chopped tomatoes
- 1 tbsp tomato paste
- 3 tsp dried oregano
- 14oz (400g) can cannellini beans, drained and rinsed
- 7oz (200g) can corn, drained and rinsed
- 3 tbsp freshly chopped parsley
- 1 cup Greek yogurt
- 1 large egg
- Small handful of vegetarian Parmesan cheese
- Salad, to serve

1 PREHEAT THE OVEN to 400°F (200°C). Heat the oil in a pan and cook the onion over medium heat for 4-5 minutes, or until it becomes soft.

2 ADD THE CHOPPED TOMATOES, tomato paste, and 1 tsp of oregano. Bring to a boil, then reduce and simmer for about 10 minutes. Stir in the beans and corn and cook for 5 minutes. Add the parsley.

3 PUT THE YOGURT, egg, and remaining 2 tsp oregano into a bowl and stir until well mixed.

4 SPOON THE BEAN MIXTURE into an ovenproof dish, then spoon the yogurt mixture on top. Sprinkle the Parmesan on top then bake in the oven for 20 minutes, or until the top is golden and set.

CORNBREAD MOUNTAIN

Boiling veggies can destroy some of the vitamins they contain, so it's best to eat them raw, steamed, or baked, like the corn in this recipe. Cornmeal is like a grainy yellow flour. It's made from ground corn kernels.

Reach for THE SKY!

Corn and cornmeal are high in fiber.

Corn is a good source of B vitamins, which help to keep the blood healthy.

10 mins   20–25 mins   Serves 9–16

INGREDIENTS

- 2 tbsp butter, for greasing
- 1 cup all-purpose flour
- ¾ cup cornmeal or polenta

- 1 tbsp baking powder
- 1 tsp salt
- 5 scallions, thinly chopped
- 1 cup drained corn
- 2 eggs
- 4 tbsp butter, melted and cooled
- 1½ cups milk

Corn contains certain B vitamins and Vitamin C.

1

PREHEAT THE OVEN to 400°F (200°C). Grease a 9in (23cm) square baking pan with butter.

2

MIX THE FLOUR, cornmeal or polenta, baking powder, salt, scallions, and corn in a large bowl.

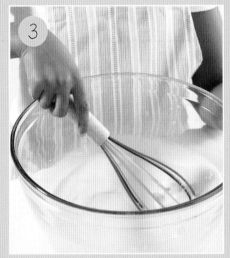

3

IN ANOTHER BOWL, whisk the eggs, cooled melted butter, and milk until thoroughly combined.

4

POUR THE WET INGREDIENTS into the dry ones and stir with a wooden spoon until everything is nicely mixed.

5

POUR THE MIXTURE into the baking pan and bake in the oven for 25–30 minutes until golden brown.

6

LET COOL before cutting into slices or squares. Cornbread makes a delicious savory snack.

SUNSHINE RICE

Rice is a hugely popular ingredient all over the world. In some countries it's eaten at every meal! Rice gives you lots of energy because it's high in carbohydrates. It goes so well with veggies!

There are lots of different types of rice. Brown rice is the best source of fiber.

Light and BRIGHT

5 mins   30 mins   Serves 4

INGREDIENTS

- 1 tbsp olive oil
- 1 onion, chopped
- 1½ cups long grain rice
- 1 tsp turmeric
- 1 green or red chile, seeded and finely chopped
- 1 large clove garlic, finely chopped
- 2½ cups hot vegetable stock
- 14oz (400g) can red kidney beans, rinsed and drained
- 3 large vine tomatoes
- 1 red and 1 green bell pepper, seeded and cubed
- 1¾oz (50g) frozen peas
- 4 scallions, chopped

Our friend turmeric is a spice that provides this dish with flavor and color. It's used as a type of medicine in parts of the world.

HEAT THE OIL in a large pan and cook the onion over low heat for 2–3 minutes until softened.

ADD THE RICE, turmeric, chile, and garlic and coat in the oil. Cook for 2 minutes, stirring constantly.

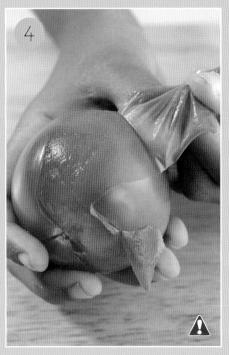

ADD THE STOCK and kidney beans to the pan and stir to combine. Cover the pan and simmer for 15 minutes, stirring occasionally.

CUT A CROSS at each end of the tomatoes and place in a bowl. Cover with boiling water for a minute then let cool. Peel off the skins, then cut into chunks and take out the seeds.

ADD THE TOMATOES, bell peppers, peas, and scallions. Cover and cook for 10 minutes more, stirring twice, until the rice has absorbed the stock and is creamy.

LEMON DRIZZLE CAKE

This lovely loaf cake is both sweet and sour at the same time. Lemons are loaded with Vitamin C, and can be a real boost to your immune system. The peel of a lemon, called the zest, is really good, too.

25 mins 45–50 mins Serves 8

INGREDIENTS

- 2 tbsp butter, for greasing
- Finely grated zest of 2 unwaxed lemons
- 14 tbsp butter, softened
- ¾ cup granulated sugar
- 3 large eggs, beaten
- 1⅓ cups self-rising flour, sifted
- 1 tsp baking powder
- 2 tbsp milk
- Juice of 2 lemons
- ⅓ cup granulated sugar
- ⅔ cup confectioners' sugar

I make the cake moist and full of yummy fresh flavor.

PREHEAT THE OVEN to 350°C (180°C). Grease a loaf pan and line the bottom with parchment paper so the cake won't stick.

PLACE THE ZEST of 2 lemons, butter, and sugar in a mixing bowl and beat until the mixture is light and fluffy.

BEAT IN THE EGGS, a little at a time. Sift the flour and baking powder together, then fold into the mixture with the milk. Put the mixture in the pan.

BAKE THE CAKE in the center of the oven for 45–50 minutes, or until a toothpick comes out clean. Prick the top of the cake with the toothpick.

MIX 4 tsp OF THE LEMON JUICE with the granulated sugar in a bowl. Drizzle the sugary juice over the cake so it sinks into the holes. Let the cake cool before turning it out of the pan.

COMBINE THE CONFECTIONERS' SUGAR with the rest of the lemon juice and mix until smooth. Drizzle the icing over the top, allowing it to run over the sides.

MEET THE ORANGES

WE'RE VIVID AND VIBRANT! The oranges rule when it comes to helping you have a healthy heart. Orange fruit and vegetables increase your immunity. The orange tribe includes tasty sweet potatoes, perfect peaches, perky pumpkins, cool carrots, brilliant butternut squash, and incredibly juicy oranges.

Big and BOLD

Eat your ORANGES

I can help to strengthen your bones and improve your digestion.

GO OVERBOARD FOR
ORANGES

Bold and brilliant, orange food tends to contain a lot of something called "beta-carotene." In your body this turns into Vitamin A, which is good for your eyes. Orange food can also contain Vitamin C, which helps protect you from illness.

PAPAYA is a fruit that grows in warm places. It's full of vitamins and minerals.

You can buy sweet potatoes that are white or orange on the inside. The orange ones taste sweeter.

Tough on the outside, but smooth and tasty on the inside. BUTTERNUT SQUASH is hearty and nutritious. Even the seeds are good for you!

SWEET
POTATO

Both potatoes and sweet potatoes are filling, packed with nutrients, and give you lots of energy, but sweet potatoes contain much more Vitamin A.

CARROTS

So much more than "rabbit food," carrots are amazing. There's an old rumor that carrots make you see in the dark. That's not exactly true, but their beta-carotene (the clue's in the name!) does help to keep your eyes healthy.

ORANGES are great as a supersweet and healthy snack.

TANGERINES are smaller and easier to peel than oranges. Both have plenty of vitamins.

Fresh APRICOTS contain useful antioxidants. Dried apricots taste great, but can contain lots of sugar.

MANGO

Known as the "king of fruit" in some parts of the world, sweet, tasty mangoes are rich in Vitamin C and beta-carotene. No wonder so many people love them!

Awesome PUMPKIN

PUMPKIN isn't just for carving at Halloween! Eating it helps to reduce blood pressure.

SWEET POTATO OMELET

Traditionally made with regular potatoes, this Spanish-style omelet, or tortilla, uses healthier sweet potatoes instead. Sweet potatoes are a versatile veggie and they taste great baked, boiled, or fried.

15 mins | **15 mins** | **Serves 4**

INGREDIENTS

- 2 sweet potatoes, 1lb (450g), peeled and sliced ¼in (5mm) thick
- 2 tbsp olive oil
- 2 tbsp butter
- 5 scallions, trimmed and chopped
- 1 yellow or orange bell pepper, seeded and sliced
- 2 tbsp fresh thyme leaves, plus extra to garnish
- Salt and freshly ground black pepper
- 6 large eggs, beaten

1. BRING WATER IN A SAUCEPAN to a boil and cook the sweet potato slices for about 5 minutes, until tender but still holding their shape. Drain carefully in a colander.

2. HEAT THE OIL and butter in a large nonstick pan. Add the scallions and bell pepper and cook over medium heat for about 2 minutes.

3. ADD THE SWEET POTATOES, thyme, salt, and pepper, then stir gently to combine. Add the eggs and cover the pan with a lid. Cook over medium-low heat for about 5 minutes, until almost set.

4. MEANWHILE, PREHEAT THE BROILER. When it's hot, put the frying pan under it for a few minutes until the egg is set and the top is golden brown. Sprinkle thyme on top and slide the omelet onto a plate.

CARROT AND ORANGE TREATS

Juicy oranges and tasty carrots are a perfect duo in this "orange" treat. Carrots contain beta-carotene, which boosts the immune system. Oranges are high in Vitamin C and A. They're good for your heart and skin.

20 mins | 25 mins | Makes 12

INGREDIENTS

- 1¼ cups all-purpose flour
- 2 tsp baking powder
- ½ tsp baking soda
- ½ cup light brown sugar
- ⅓ cup hazelnuts, chopped
- 1 tbsp poppy seeds
- 1 carrot, 3½ oz (100g), grated
- ⅓ cup golden raisins
- ½ tsp ground cinnamon
- 1¼ cups rolled oats
- Zest and juice of 1 large orange
- ¾ cup buttermilk
- 1 large egg, beaten
- 5 tbsp butter, melted
- Pinch of salt

The top has a golden brown crunchy texture... ready and waiting for you to dive in. Yum!

1. PREHEAT THE OVEN to 400°F (200°C). In a large bowl, combine the flour, baking powder, baking soda, and sugar. Stir in the nuts, poppy seeds, carrot, golden raisins, cinnamon, oats, and orange zest.

2. IN A SECOND BOWL, mix the buttermilk, egg, butter, salt, and orange juice. Mix with a spatula, then pour the wet ingredients into the dry.

3. USE A SPATULA to fold the mixture together gently. Be careful not to mix the batter too much, or the muffins won't end up light and fluffy.

4. LINE MUFFIN PANS with 12 paper liners, then spoon the mixture into the liners—filling them two-thirds of the way full. Bake for 20–25 minutes. Transfer to a wire rack to cool.

BUTTERNUT SQUASH SOUP

There's nothing else like a tasty bowl of soup on a chilly day. The smaller a squash is the more flavor it will have, so don't always choose the biggest one. Butternut squash is similar to pumpkin. Did you know they're both fruits, not vegetables?

Orange bell peppers are full of Vitamins A and C. The Vitamin C content is highest when the pepper is ripe.

1, 2, 3... ...LIFT!

Butternut squash contains many different vitamins and minerals, as well as lots of fiber. It releases energy slowly and keeps your blood sugar levels stable.

15 mins | 40 mins | Serves 4

INGREDIENTS

- 2¼lb (1kg) butternut squash
- 2 medium carrots, approximately 7oz (200g)
- 1 orange bell pepper, seeded and chopped
- 1 tbsp vegetable oil
- 1 onion, coarsely chopped
- 4 cups vegetable stock
- Roasted pumpkin seeds (optional)

Put your back into it guys!

1 PREHEAT THE OVEN to 400°F (200°C). Cut the butternut squash in half lengthwise and scoop out the seeds and pith from the center.

2 CAREFULLY REMOVE the skin with a peeler. Cut the squash into small cubes about ¾in (2cm) in size. Peel and coarsely chop the carrots.

3 PLACE THE PEPPER, carrots, and squash cubes in a baking pan and drizzle oil on top. Season with salt and pepper, then roast for 20 minutes.

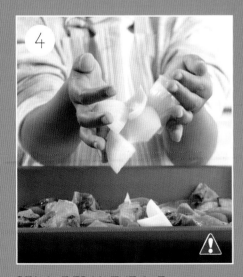

4 REMOVE FROM THE OVEN and add the onion. Return the baking pan to the oven for another 15 minutes. Remove and let cool slightly.

5 PLACE THE VEGETABLES and half the stock in a food processor and blend until smooth. Or you can mash the squash with a potato masher.

6 POUR THE MIXTURE back into a saucepan, add the rest of the stock, and simmer for 3–4 minutes, until hot. Serve with a sprinkling of pumpkin seeds on top.

MANGO AND COCONUT POPS

Mangoes are naturally sweet and full of fiber, copper, and Vitamin C. These refreshing little popsicles are the perfect treat on a hot summer day.

2–3 hours   0 mins   Makes 6–8

INGREDIENTS

- 1 ripe mango
- 14 fl oz (400ml) can coconut milk
- 2 tbsp honey
- Juice of 2 limes

Super CHILLED!

Coconut milk is really nutritious. Coconuts are high in fiber and contain lots of vitamins and minerals.

1

ASK AN ADULT to slice the lobes off the mango, guiding the knife around the pit in the middle.

2

SCORE A DIAMOND crisscross pattern on the lobes, then turn it inside out to create a hedgehog shape from the mango chunks. Cut off the mango chunks.

3

PLACE THE MANGO, coconut milk, honey, and lime juice in a blender and blend until smooth.

4

POUR THE MIX into popsicle molds, but don't fill them all the way to the top. Place a stick in the middle of each one and freeze for 2–3 hours.

INDEX

Eat me again soon!

DK WOULD LIKE TO THANK

Caryn Jenner for proofreading. Eleanor Bates, Rachael Hare, Charlotte Milner, and Artie the dog for help with photoshoots. Sadie Thomas for the illustrations. Lucy Claxton and Laura Evans for picture library assistance. Barney Allen, Lindsay Guzman, Egypt Hanson, Rio Lewis, Grace Merchant, Liberty Moore, and Olivia Phokou for modeling.

ACKNOWLEDGMENTS

The publisher would like to thank the following for their kind permission to reproduce their photographs:

(Key: a-above; b-below/bottom; c-center; f-far; l-left; r-right; t-top)

14 Joanne Duran (c) Dorling Kindersley, Courtesy of RHS Hampton Court Flower Show 2011

All other images © Dorling Kindersley

For further information see: www.dkimages.com